# Hymns
## for
# Personal
# Devotions

# Hymns for Personal Devotions

Compiled and Annotated by
## Jerry B. Jenkins

**MOODY PRESS**
CHICAGO

ISBN: 0-8024-3836-9

2 3 4 5 6 7 8 Printing/AK/Year 94 93 92 91 90

*Printed in the United States of America*

*To my mother,*
*who couldn't make me stick with piano lessons*
*but nonetheless gave me a lifelong appreciation*
*for music*

# Contents

# Introduction
# "Sing to Deity"

As a magazine editor, I once bought from a young woman a story that was neither dramatic nor sensational, but which reached me.

She wrote of having been on a long college choir tour. By the evening of the last concert, the students had seen an exciting adventure deteriorate into a grueling ordeal. Short of sleep and patience, they bickered and gossiped.

The director, perhaps sensing their fatigue, encouraged them, "Tonight, sing to Deity."

As they donned robes and lined up to proceed onto the platform, the girl wondered, *What does that mean, sing to Deity? He wants us to sing to God instead of to the audience.*

That sounded all right to her. As she positioned herself on the front row she knew that after a couple of dozen concerts, the memorized songs had become meaningless to her. By focusing on a new audience, an audience of One, she would have to concentrate on the lyrics.

From the first note of a worship anthem, she was unable to sing. Merely thinking of the beautiful words of love and devotion to Christ caused tears to well up and cascade down her face. She mouthed the text, ignorant of the human audience, praying it to God.

The experience convicted her of pettiness, of jealousy, of backbiting. All this she confessed as she sang. During intermission she asked forgiveness from people for whom she had harbored bad feelings. Then she tried to pull herself together, hoping to be able to sing during the second half of the program.

But when she tried, her heart pure and her mind uncluttered, she found herself even more overwhelmed with love and gratitude to God. She wept through the end of the concert, still only mouthing the words, unable to sing. Many in the audience told her director that her emotion had been contagious and had ministered to them.

There is something deeply moving about music written not simply about God, but *to* Him. I love gospel songs and choruses, those that deal with our relationship to Christ, what He has done for us, and what awaits us in heaven. But even more meaningful to me are hymns that address God personally. They are written to be sung vertically. These are works not primarily for the edification of the believer; they are gifts of worship to the King.

9

Of course, such expressions *are* wonderfully inspiring to the worshiper. Much can be learned and gained from such beautiful modes of devotion. Some of the great hymns of the faith seem almost divinely inspired.

The hymn texts in this volume are designed for use in your personal devotions. Regardless what else you do during your quiet time, and whether it's daily or weekly or somewhere in between, this handbook may be used in addition.

The texts are so familiar that I didn't feel it necessary to provide the music. My hope is that you recognize every selection at first glance, by title alone. You may not need even the lyrics for many of them. You may want to hum while reading the words, or you may want to sing softly, or even aloud. You need not be able to carry a tune. These are not for performing. They are solely for expressing your devotion to God in a form beautiful to Him.

You might want to consider this the dessert portion of your devotional meal. After you've read the milk of the Word, studied the meat of the Word, prayed and listened for the voice of God to your own spirit, you can finish by lifting a hymn of praise to Him.

I have selected fifty-two hymns, one for each week of the year. I recommend singing the same one every day for a week. After just a few times, you will have it memorized, and by singing it repeatedly before moving onto the next, you'll discover something new in it each time. If you have become rusty or inconsistent in your daily quiet times, these hymns may provide a convenient way to get back on track.

Though I do not see these as complete devotionals in themselves, sincerely and prayerfully singing one to God each day is certainly better than ignoring Him altogether. My hope is that these texts will become more meaningful to you every time you sing them, that they will be an enriching addition to your devotional life, and that you'll draw closer to God through worshiping Him.

The book itself has been designed to take with you wherever you go. Don't give up if you miss a day or two, or even a week or two. This is a book easy to come back to.

I hope it becomes a friendly companion and supports your effort to praise God.

JERRY B. JENKINS
Chicago

# 1

*Holy, Holy, Holy*
*More Love to Thee*
*O Love That Will Not Let Me Go*
*Breathe on Me, Breath of God*

**W**hat better way to begin a musical journey to devotion than with the beautiful and haunting *Holy, Holy, Holy.* This has been a favorite of Christians for ages because of its reverent and prayerful tone.

As an adult I have sung this with congregations who enjoy an up-tempo pace, brightly chorusing phrases like "Early in the morning, my song shall rise to Thee!" I will never forget, however, the way I learned it as a child at the little Oakwood Bible Church in Kalamazoo, Michigan. There we sang it prayerfully and *very* slowly.

Try it. It may take a little work to slow yourself, but these are words rich and deep in meaning. Majestic superlatives and phrasing like "Perfect in power, in love, and purity" demand thought and reflection.

Tomorrow or the next day, you may want to sing this hymn with gusto and speed. Or you may become addicted to it in a deliberate, prayer-like pace, as I have. Follow your own urgings, but digest every word. This is one you may come back to frequently.

# Holy, Holy, Holy
### *Reginald Heber*

Holy, Holy, Holy! Lord God Almighty!
Early in the morning my song shall rise to Thee;
Holy, Holy, Holy! Merciful and Mighty!
God in Three Persons, blessed Trinity!

Holy, Holy, Holy! All the saints adore Thee,
Casting down their golden crowns around the glassy sea;
Cherubim and seraphim falling down before Thee,
Which were and art, and evermore shalt be.

Holy, Holy, Holy! Tho' the darkness hide Thee,
Tho' the eye of sinful man Thy glory may not see,
Only Thou art holy; there is none beside Thee
Perfect in power, in love, and purity.

Holy, Holy, Holy! Lord God Almighty!
All Thy works shall praise Thy name, in earth, and sky,
    and sea;
Holy, Holy, Holy! Merciful and Mighty!
God in Three Persons, blessed Trinity!

**M**_ore Love to Thee_ is more than an acceptable prayer directed to Christ. As you mull over these lyrics you'll see that it is no empty sentiment. The writer refers to sorrow, grief, and pain as sweet messengers that lead her to more love for Christ.

Having given up on the "earthly joy" she craved and the peace and rest she sought, now all she seeks is Christ. She pleads with Him to "give what is best."

Elizabeth P. Prentiss and her husband, a minister, lost two children in less than a year. Beside herself with grief, she journaled, "A bleeding, fainting, broken heart, this is my gift to Thee."

My father, a policeman, has said that praying is like looking down the barrel of a loaded gun. You may get what you ask for. Can we honestly pray in song that God will "let sorrow do its work" in our lives?

# More Love to Thee

*Elizabeth P. Prentiss*

More love to Thee, O Christ, more love to Thee!
Hear Thou the prayer I make on bended knee;
This is my earnest plea: More love, O Christ, to Thee,
More love to Thee, more love to Thee!

Once earthly joy I craved, sought peace and rest;
Now Thee alone I seek, give what is best;
This all my prayer shall be: More love, O Christ, to Thee,
More love to Thee, more love to Thee!

Let sorrow do its work, send grief and pain;
Sweet are Thy messengers, sweet their refrain,
When they can sing with me: More love, O Christ, to Thee,
More love to Thee, more love to Thee!

Then shall my latest breath whisper Thy praise;
This be the parting cry my heart shall raise;
This still its prayer shall be: More love, O Christ, to Thee,
More love to Thee, more love to Thee!

**G**eorge Matheson wrote *O Love That Wilt Not Let Me Go* in language reminiscent of the King James Version of the Bible, but don't miss the wonderful metaphors that characterize his deep relationship with God.

Matheson, of poor eyesight from childhood and blind by age eighteen, says he wrote this hymn in 1882 as the fruit of "severe mental suffering" over a disappointment in his life.

He offers back to God "the life I owe" and compares his thus richer and fuller life in Christ to "Thine ocean depths." His feeling of debt makes me think of the simple, yet deeply profound modern chorus that says, "He paid a debt He did not owe, I owed a debt I could not pay...."

Matheson's "flickering torch" is compared to God's "sunshine blaze," his painful hope to a rainbow, and life's glory is laid dead in the dust while from the ground blossoms forth endless life.

These lyrics are worth the time to work through the archaic phrases. As you sing it each day you'll see similarities to *More Love to Thee,* especially where the writer refers to joy that "seekest me through pain." We can't sing great hymns of love and devotion to God without sensing the price of fellowship with Him.

# O Love That Wilt Not Let Me Go

*George Matheson*

O Love that wilt not let me go, I rest my weary soul in
    Thee;
I give Thee back the life I owe,
That in Thine ocean depths its flow may richer, fuller be.

O Light that followest all my way, I yield my flickering
    torch to Thee;
My heart restores its borrowed ray,
That in Thy sunshine's blaze its day may brighter, fairer be.

O Joy that seekest me through pain, I cannot close my
    heart to Thee;
I trace the rainbow through the rain,
And feel the promise is not vain that morn shall tearless be.

O Cross that liftest up my head, I dare not ask to fly from
    Thee;
I lay in dust life's glory dead,
And from the ground there blossoms red life that shall
    endless be.

**P**rayer warriors, those who have given themselves to communion with God and can be called "men and women of prayer," have learned the truth of not just talking to God, but also of listening for His voice.

I do not count myself among that number, but it is a worthy goal. I have known some great people of prayer: Evangelist Sammy Tippit, a Romanian layman named Titus, the late Chinese saint Christiana Tsai, and Pastor Bill Hybels.

These learned to wait upon God, spending hours communing with Him, letting Him deeply impress their spirits. Titus, the Romanian, once prayed in Sammy Tippit's hearing that "if it takes the blood of the martyrs to reach my people for Christ, let me be the first to shed blood."

Such a prayer comes from the heart of one who has learned, as the writer of this week's hymn learned, to seek the breath of God on his life.

*Breathe on Me, Breath of God* can be sung in a whisper. Don't miss studying the phrasings that, even in fragments, paint vivid pictures. For instance, the last phrase of each of the four short verses can be combined to form this line: "fill me with life anew, until my heart is pure, till I am wholly Thine, so shall I never die."

# Breathe on Me, Breath of God

*Edwin Hatch*

Breathe on me, Breath of God, fill me with life anew,
That I may love what Thou dost love, and do what Thou
  wouldst do.

Breathe on me, Breath of God, until my heart is pure,
Until with Thee I will one will, to do and to endure.

Breathe on me, Breath of God, till I am wholly Thine,
Until this earthly part of me glows with Thy fire divine.

Breathe on me, Breath of God, so shall I never die,
But live with Thee the perfect life of Thine eternity.

# 2

*O God, Our Help in Ages Past*
*Praise Him! Praise Him!*
*Whiter Than Snow*
*Amazing Grace*

**L**est you think a hymn with the title *O God, Our Help in Ages Past* is a relic harking back to days of old, concentrate on the phrase "our hope for years to come." Though Isaac Watts wrote it in the early 1700s, it has stood for more than two centuries as what hymnologist Kenneth W. Osbeck calls a "grand commentary on the whole subject of time."

This is a hymn that can be sung only in deepest humility. I always feel as if I am singing with the great host of saints who have gone on before, especially considering that the text has been adapted from Psalm 90, a psalm of Moses.

The imagery of God as not only our help and shelter and hope and guide, but also as our *home* is deeply meaningful. What comes to mind when you think of home? Do you think of love and warmth and family? Do you recall your childhood or dwell on the present?

Perhaps your memories of home are painful. Watts' reference to God Himself as our eternal home evokes emotions so ideal that whether our concept of home is disturbing or wonderful, what we have to look forward to is far better.

# O God, Our Help in Ages Past
*Isaac Watts*

O God, our help in ages past, my hope for years to come,
My shelter from the stormy blast, and my eternal home!

Under the shadow of Thy throne, still may I dwell secure;
Sufficient is Thine arm alone, and my defense is sure.

Before the hills in order stood, or earth received her
 frame,
From everlasting Thou art God, to endless years the same.

A thousand ages, in Thy sight, are like an evening gone;
Short as the watch that ends the night, before the rising
 sun.

O God, our help in ages past, my hope for years to come,
Be Thou my guide while life shall last, and my eternal
 home.

**A**re you in the mood for a bright, uplifting song of praise? There's no one like the beloved, blind hymnwriter Fanny Crosby to provide the lyrics. The memories of this hymn take me back to Sunday morning worship services where we always stood to sing *Praise Him! Praise Him!*

This is another of those, however, that can take on new meaning if you vary your approach to it every other day or so. Sing it standing, at full volume and quick pace, the first time. Then try it on your knees, enunciated slowly and softly, focusing on each word.

Years ago a pop tune called "Breakin' Up Is Hard To Do" raced to the top of the charts as a fast-paced, soft-rock hit. More than a decade later the same composer/singer sang the same song as a slow ballad, and it rocketed to fame again. The new treatment gave the lyric a whole new feel and meaning.

If that can happen with a ditty about human love, imagine the experience of recasting this bright praise hymn as a private worship prayer. Miss Crosby has infused the text with theology, doctrine, and metaphors bearing the entire truth of the gospel.

# Praise Him! Praise Him!

*Fanny J. Crosby*

Praise Him! praise Him! Jesus, my blessed Redeemer!
Sing, O Earth, His wonderful love proclaim!
Hail Him! hail Him! highest archangels in glory;
Strength and honor give to His holy name!
Like a shepherd Jesus will guard His children,
In His arms He carries them all day long:

*Refrain:*
Praise Him! praise Him! tell of His excellent greatness;
Praise Him! praise Him! ever in joyful song!

Praise Him! praise Him! Jesus, my blessed Redeemer!
For my sins He suffered, and bled and died;
He my Rock, my hope of eternal salvation,
Hail Him! hail Him! Jesus the Crucified.
Sound His praises! Jesus who bore my sorrows;
Love unbounded, wonderful, deep and strong:

*Refrain*

Praise Him! praise Him! Jesus, my blessed Redeemer!
Heavenly portals loud with hosannas ring!
Jesus, Savior, reigneth forever and ever;
Crown Him! crown Him! Prophet and Priest and King!
Christ is coming! over the world victorious,
Power and glory unto the Lord belong:

*Refrain*

**R**egardless the state of our spiritual temperature, *Whiter than Snow* may be sung with all sincerity. Unless you have reached a state of sinless perfection (I sure haven't!), you can sing with James Nicholson, "Lord Jesus, I long to be perfectly whole."

This is a prayer sung directly to Christ, and it can be a convicting experience. We want Him forever to live in our souls, but do we really want him to break down *every* idol? Are we willing to make a complete sacrifice? To give up ourselves and *whatever* we know?

*Whiter than Snow* is a song of salvation, and it's likely that if this book is something you enjoy, you are already saved. Yet what a reminder of what we have in Him! And what an opportunity to perhaps pray this sincerely for the first time in your life.

Through this hymn we can, with the psalmist, pray, "Create in me a new heart, O God."

# Whiter than Snow

*James Nicholson*

Lord Jesus, I long to be perfectly whole;
I want Thee forever to live in my soul;
Break down every idol, cast out every foe;
Now wash me, and I shall be whiter than snow.

*Refrain*:
Whiter than snow, yes, whiter than snow;
Now wash me, and I shall be whiter than snow.

Lord Jesus, look down from Thy throne in the skies,
And help me to make a complete sacrifice;
I give up myself, and whatever I know,
Now wash me, and I shall be whiter than snow.

*Refrain*

Lord Jesus, for this I most humbly entreat,
I want, blessed Lord, at Thy crucified feet;
By faith, for my cleansing, I see Thy blood flow,
Now wash me, and I shall be whiter than snow.

*Refrain*

Lord Jesus, Thou seest I patiently wait,
Come now, and within me a new heart create;
To those who have sought Thee, Thou never saidst "No,"
Now wash me, and I shall be whiter than snow.

*Refrain*

**O**ne of the most famous and favored works in all of hymnody, *Amazing Grace,* was penned by John Newton in the 1700s. It is consistently listed with *The Old Rugged Cross* as the most beloved hymns of all time.

The simple form tells a story of salvation and growth in Christ, which reflects the writer's own pilgrimage. Newton had been a slave shipper before reading Thomas a Kempis's *Imitation of Christ* and eventually becoming a Christian.

Though it is my wife's favorite, this hymn is so familiar that I debated including it. Even singing it slowly and meditatively for several days may not break through your barrier of intimacy with the lyric. If you find that true, try these three verses that are seldom included in hymnals.

> The Lord has promised good to me, His
>     Word my hope secures;
> He will my shield and portion be as long as
>     life endures.
>
> Yes, when this heart and flesh shall fail, and
>     mortal life shall cease,
> I shall possess within the veil, a life of joy
>     and peace.
>
> The earth shall soon dissolve like snow, the
>     sun forbear to shine;
> But God, who called me here below, will
>     be forever mine.

# Amazing Grace!
# How Sweet the Sound
*John Newton*

Amazing grace! how sweet the sound, that saved a wretch
like me!
I once was lost, but now am found, was blind, but now I
see.

'Twas grace that taught my heart to fear, and grace my
fears relieved;
How precious did that grace appear the hour I first
believed!

Through many dangers, toils and snares, I have already
come;
'Tis grace hath brought me safe thus far, and grace will
lead me home.

When I've been there ten thousand years, bright shining
as the sun,
I've no less days to sing God's praise than when I first
begun.

# 3

*Search Me, O God*
*The Church's One Foundation*
*I Will Sing the Wondrous Story*
*Beneath the Cross of Jesus*

**S**earch Me, O God is a simple song, with a simple message, and a simple tune. There is a problem with it, however. Its truth, its petition, is anything but simple.

This hymn departs slightly from the approach of the others in this collection because it is not a pure worship vehicle. Rather than lavishing praise upon God for one or more of His many attributes, we are led here to seek the searchlight of His truth upon our hearts.

It fits a worship ensemble, of course, because wishing to be rid of every sin and being set free is honoring to God. Don't miss the one, brief line of pure praise, "I praise Thee, Lord, for cleansing me of sin, fulfill Thy Word and make me pure within."

When we acknowledge that our purity is a fulfillment of God's Word and will, we put ourselves in a position to be examined by the only great Judge of the universe. Suddenly the song with the simple tune and message is an ominous petition.

Only with pure hearts can we sing, "Grant my desire to magnify Thy name." Here is a hymn that requires honesty and humility before the Lord. It would be a mistake to sing it without deep thought.

# Search Me, O God

*J. Edwin Orr*

Search me, O God, and know my heart today;
Try me, O Savior, know my thoughts, I pray.
See if there be some wicked way in me;
Cleanse me from every sin and set me free.

I praise Thee, Lord, for cleansing me from sin;
Fulfill Thy Word and make me pure within.
Fill me with fire where once I burned with shame;
Grant my desire to magnify Thy name.

Lord, take my life and make it wholly Thine;
Fill my poor heart with Thy great love divine.
Take all my will, my passion, self and pride;
I now surrender, Lord—in me abide.

O Holy Spirit, revival comes from Thee;
Send a revival—start the work in me.
Thy Word declares Thou wilt supply our need;
For blessings now, O Lord, I humbly plead.

**Y**ou cannot sing *The Church's One Foundation* without immediately realizing that this is not a typical worship hymn. It's a standard, a widely-used favorite, an anthem heard in Sunday morning services all over the world.

But clearly this is a hymn of doctrine and theology. Indeed, the lyricist was a Church of England pastor with a clear agenda. Every line, every word is designed to support the ninth article of the Apostle's Creed, which states: "The Holy Catholic (Universal) Church; the Communion of Saints: He is the Head of this Body."

In 1866, when this hymn was written (along with eleven others, one for each of the articles of the Creed), the Church was in the midst of a liberal/conservative controversy. The literality of Scripture was in question, and Samuel J. Stone felt the attacks of liberals and modern scholars might segment and eventually destroy the church.

That background in no way diminishes the impact and benefit of this piece of music as a personal expression of devotion and praise to God. In fact, if studied carefully with Scripture passages (start with Ephesians 5:23), the Apostle's Creed, and a commentary, it becomes a profound learning experience.

# The Church's One Foundation

*Samuel J. Stone*

The Church's one Foundation is Jesus Christ her Lord;
She is His new creation, by water and the word:
From heaven He came and sought her to be His holy
    bride;
With His own blood He bought her, and for her life He
    died.

Elect from every nation, yet one o'er all the earth,
Her charter of salvation, one Lord, one faith, one birth;
One holy name she blesses, partakes one holy food,
And to one hope she presses, with every grace endued.

'Mid toil and tribulation, and tumult of her war,
She waits the consummation of peace forevermore;
Till with the vision glorious her longing eyes are blest,
And the great Church victorious shall be the Church at
    rest.

Yet she on earth hath union with God the Three in One,
And mystic sweet communion with those whose rest is
    won:
O happy ones and holy! Lord, give us grace that we,
Like them, the meek and lowly, on high may dwell with
    Thee.

**I**n one of the churches of my youth was a men's quartet that sang wonderful, harmonious oldies like *On the Jericho Road; Over in the Glory Land; There's a New Name Written Down in Glory;* and one that fits an assortment like the one you hold in your hands: *I Will Sing the Wondrous Story.*

I can't sing it without remembering that band of blue collar workers, of whom three couldn't read a note of music. They occasionally practiced at our home, where my mother—the choir director—coached and accompanied them. They loved to sing, and though they seldom sang outside our church, I know others would have enjoyed them, too.

If this song is as familiar to you as it is to me, you'll recall the delightful echoes in the chorus: "Yes, I'll sing (Yes, I'll sing) the wondrous story (the wondrous story) of the Christ (of the Christ) who died for me (who died for me). . . ."

As this book is intended for personal, private devotions, do what I do with this song: sing both parts. I always wanted to be a bass, and though my lowest note is still several notes higher than would be acceptable in four-part harmony, I take a shot at it anyway.

This is a song to sing to God about His Son. It's fun and it moves, and by the end of the week, it'll move you, too.

# I Will Sing the Wondrous Story

*Francis H. Rowley*

I will sing the wondrous story of the Christ who died for
    me,
How He left His home in glory for the cross of Calvary.

*Refrain*:
Yes, I'll sing the wondrous story of the Christ who died
    for me,
Sing it with the saints in glory, gathered by the crystal sea.

I was lost, but Jesus found me, found the sheep that went
    astray,
Threw his loving arms around me, drew me back into His
    way.

*Refrain*

I was bruised, but Jesus healed me; faint was I from many
    a fall;
Sight was gone, and fears possessed me, but He freed me
    from them all.

*Refrain*

Days of darkness still come o'er me, sorrow's paths I often
    tread,
But the Savior still is with me; by His hand I'm safely led.

*Refrain*

He will keep me till the river rolls its waters at my feet;
Then He'll bear me safely over, where the loved ones I
    shall meet.

*Refrain*

**B**eneath the Cross of Jesus is an appropriate coun-
terbalance to the hymn that precedes it. Here is a slow,
plaintive declaration of personal faith that draws upon
countless passages of Scripture (mostly Old Testament) to
make its point.

The six metaphors in the first stanza alone can be
traced to such passages as Isaiah 32:2, Psalm 63:1, Jeremiah
9:2, Isaiah 28:12, Isaiah 4:6, and Matthew 11:30.

I appreciate especially the reference in the last verse
to the shadow of the cross as "my abiding place." Even
people who crave the sunlight and are depressed on
cloudy days can sing with Elizabeth Clephane, "I ask no
other sunshine than the sunshine of His face."

Some think references to ourselves as "wretches" (as
in Amazing Grace) and "my sinful self" (as in this hymn)
are not psychologically healthy. Yet the true believer,
aware of his shortcomings, must know that spiritually he
is worthless, even dead, aside from the work of Christ on
the cross. That knowledge makes the last line all the more
meaningful:

"Content to let the world go by, to know no gain nor
loss, my sinful self my only shame, my glory all the cross."

# Beneath the Cross of Jesus

*Elizabeth C. Clephane*

Beneath the cross of Jesus I fain would take my stand—
The shadow of a mighty Rock within a weary land;
A home within the wilderness, a rest upon the way,
From the burning of the noontide heat, and the burden of
the day.

Upon that cross of Jesus mine eye at times can see
The very dying form of One who suffered there for me;
And from my smitten heart with tears two wonders I
    confess—
The wonders of redeeming love and my unworthiness.

I take, O cross, thy shadow for my abiding place;
I ask no other sunshine than the sunshine of His face;
Content to let the world go by, to know no gain nor loss,
My sinful self my only shame, my glory all the cross.

# 4

*To God Be the Glory*
*When I Survey the Wondrous Cross*
*There Is a Fountain*
*In the Cross of Christ I Glory*

**T**o *God Be the Glory* is a fitting way to start this foursome of hymns which increasingly centers on the work of Christ on the cross.

Written by Fanny Crosby, this bright expression of praise is all the more eloquent because it was written by a woman who, because of her blindness, could have wallowed in bitterness and self-pity.

Instead, she plainly outlines the gospel in the first verse and follows with a refrain worthy of the King. Near the end of the second verse she again reminds us of our lowly spiritual state outside the love of God ("The vilest offender...."), and exults in the promise that if we truly believe, "that moment from Jesus" a pardon we receive.

Don't miss the poignant last line of the third stanza, in which the sightless poet writes, "But purer, and higher, and greater will be my wonder, my transport, when Jesus we see."

# To God Be the Glory

*Fanny J. Crosby*

To God be the glory, great things He hath done,
So loved He the world that He gave us His Son,
Who yielded His life an atonement for sin,
And opened the Lifegate that all may go in.

*Refrain*:
Praise the Lord, praise the Lord, let the earth hear His
    voice!
Praise the Lord, praise the Lord, let the people rejoice!
O come to the Father thro' Jesus the Son,
And give Him the glory, great things He hath done.

O perfect redemption, the purchase of blood,
To ev'ry believer the promise of God;
The vilest offender who truly believes,
That moment from Jesus a pardon receives.

*Refrain*

Great things He hath taught us, great things He hath done,
And great our rejoicing thro' Jesus the Son;
But purer, and higher, and greater will be
Our wonder, our transport, when Jesus we see.

*Refrain*

**I**f I had to select my favorite from this entire collection, it might be Isaac Watts's melancholy *When I Survey the Wondrous Cross.* I can't count the times this hymn has so moved me to tears that I could only mouth the words with the congregation.

This is a masterpiece that washes over us, portraying the suffering of the Prince of glory in graphic detail, pushing us to count our richest gain but loss and to pour contempt on our pride. "All the vain things that charm me most, I sacrifice them to His blood."

Perhaps it's the distance between where Watts encourages me to be and where I truly am that makes this hymn so hard to sing. It's a lofty and worthy spiritual goal to say that "Love so amazing, so divine, demands my soul, my life, my all," but how short I fall!

In my opinion, the third verse of this brief but poignant work rivals the third verse of *It Is Well with My Soul* as the greatest in all of hymnody. Though that selection does not appear here, it's worth looking up for an enriching time of reflection.

# When I Survey
# the Wondrous Cross
*Isaac Watts*

When I survey the wondrous cross, on which the Prince
of glory died,
My richest gain I count but loss, and pour contempt on all
my pride.

Forbid it, Lord, that I should boast, save in the death of
Christ, my God;
All the vain things that charm me most, I sacrifice them to
His blood.

See, from His head, His hands, His feet, sorrow and love
flow mingled down;
Did e'er such love and sorrow meet, or thorns compose
so rich a crown?

Were the whole realm of nature mine, that were a present
far too small;
Love so amazing, so divine, demands my soul, my life, my
all.

**W**illiam Cowper's *There Is a Fountain* suffers from the same image problem as does a modern gospel song by Andre Crouch: *The Blood Will Never Lose Its Power.* Critics say both are gory and overblown in their imagery, Crouch's for his picture of blood that reaches to the highest mountain and flows to the deepest valley, and Cowper's for his fountain filled with blood, drawn from Immanuel's veins. "And sinners plunged beneath that flood lose all their guilty stains. . . ."

I don't have a problem with either offering, preferring to meditate on the effect of the blood on the stain of sin rather than on imagining literal fountains and rivers of blood.

Cowper's is another of those hymns that can be sung slowly and deliberately to elicit the richest meaning from each word. His text is repetitious for the sake of emphasis, and is based on Zechariah 13:1. Once you have sung the second line of each stanza, the rest of the verse repeats that truth until it is burnished on your mind.

# There Is a Fountain
*William Cowper*

There is a fountain filled with blood drawn from
    Immanuel's veins;
And sinners, plunged beneath that flood, lose all their
    guilty stains:
Lose all their guilty stains, lose all their guilty stains;
And sinners, plunged beneath that flood, lose all their
    guilty stains.

The dying thief rejoiced to see that fountain in his day;
And there may I, though vile as he, wash all my sins away:
Wash all my sins away, wash all my sins away;
And there may I, though vile as he, wash all my sins away.

Dear dying Lamb, Thy precious blood shall never lose its
    power,
Till all the ransomed Church of God be saved, to sin no
    more:
Be saved, to sin no more, be saved, to sin no more;
Till all the ransomed Church of God be saved, to sin no
    more.

E'er since by faith I saw the stream Thy flowing wounds
    supply,
Redeeming love has been my theme, and shall be till I die:
And shall be till I die, and shall be till I die;
Redeeming love has been my theme, and shall be till I die.

When this poor lisping, stammering tongue lies silent in
    the grave,
Then in a nobler, sweeter song, I'll sing Thy power to
    save:
I'll sing Thy power to save, I'll sing Thy power to save;
Then in a nobler, sweeter song I'll sing Thy power to save.

**O**ften the shortest works are the most meaningful, and this is true of *In the Cross of Christ* by John Bowring. I enjoy it nearly as much as my favorite, *When I Survey the Wondrous Cross,* and there are many similarities. Four brief couplets pack so much reality and emotion that if the work were any longer it might be less effective. To me it's like a rich dessert.

Legend has it that the writer, upon a visit to the China coast, was impressed by a huge cross that remained standing on what was left of a great cathedral after a typhoon. Thus the opening line about the cross "standing o'er the wrecks of time."

Here again is a hymn that fits our criteria, if it is sung to God as a tribute of thanks for the gift of His Son.

# In the Cross of Christ I Glory

*John Bowring*

In the cross of Christ I glory, towering o'er the wrecks of
  time;
All the light of sacred story gathers round its head
  sublime.

When the woes of life o'ertake me, hopes deceive, and
  fears annoy,
Never shall the cross forsake me: Lo! it glows with peace
  and joy.

When the sun of bliss is beaming light and love upon my
  way,
From the cross the radiance streaming adds more luster
  to the day.

Bane and blessing, pain and pleasure, by the cross are
  sanctified;
Peace is there that knows no measure, joys that through
  all time abide.

# 5

*Guide Me, O Thou Great Jehovah*
*Glorious Things of Thee Are Spoken*
*I Surrender All*
*O Happy Day*

**T**hough written in the 1700s, the majestic *Guide Me, O Thou Great Jehovah* remains a stirring anthem enjoyed in seventy-five languages. If I were to choose an archetypical hymn to represent the criteria for inclusion in this volume, *Guide Me . . .* would be the perfect choice.

I have the unusual privilege of attending chapel once a week in the Torrey-Gray Auditorium at the Moody Bible Institute. Students, faculty, and staff provide lofty congregational singing, two thousand voices raised in thrilling praise. It always reminds me of my first night as a seventeen-year-old freshman in 1967 when my new classmates and I jammed the tiny Alumni Auditorium and introduced ourselves to each other.

And then we sang. Great hymns of the faith that transported us back to our homes and churches echoed through that small assembly hall. *Guide Me . . .* was one of the greatest, with its myriad Old Testament word pictures referring to God as the Bread of heaven, the strong Deliverer, my strength and shield, the Death of death, and hell's destruction.

Clearly this hymn was meant to be sung at full power in a corporate setting, but it can also be whispered reverently for profound personal impact. "Songs of praises, songs of praises, I will ever give to Thee. I will ever give to Thee."

# Guide Me, O Thou Great Jehovah
*William Williams*

Guide me, O Thou great Jehovah, pilgrim through this
    barren land;
I am weak, but Thou art mighty; hold me with Thy
    powerful hand;
Bread of heaven, Bread of heaven, feed me till I want no
    more,
Feed me till I want no more.

Open now the crystal fountain, whence the healing
    stream doth flow;
Let the fire and cloudy pillar lead me all my journey
    through;
Strong Deliverer, strong Deliverer, be Thou still my
    strength and shield,
Be Thou still my strength and shield.

When I tread the verge of Jordan, bid my anxious fears
    subside;
Death of death, and hell's destruction, land me safe on
    Canaan's side;
Songs of praises, songs of praises I will ever give to Thee.
I will ever give to Thee.

**A**nother hymn with delightful Old Testament images is *Glorious Things of Thee Are Spoken,* written by John Newton, author of *Amazing Grace.* I especially appreciate the thought referring to the stream of living water in the previous line, "Who can faint, when such a river flows their thirst to assuage?"

When this hymn was first published, in part one of the Olney Hymns *Hymnal* in 1779, it also contained these two final stanzas, usually not found in modern compilations:

> Savior, if of Zion's city I through grace a
>     member am,
> Let the world deride or pity, I will glory in
>     Thy name;
> Fading is the worlding's pleasure, all his
>     boasted pomp and show;
> Solid joys and lasting treasure, none but
>     Zion's children know.
>
> Blest inhabitants of Zion, washed in the
>     Redeemer's blood!
> Jesus, whom their souls rely on, makes
>     them kings and priests to God.
> 'Tis His love His people raises, over self to
>     reign as kings,
> And as priests, His solemn praises each for a
>     thank-off'ring brings.

# Glorious Things of Thee Are Spoken

*John Newton*

Glorious things of thee are spoken, Zion, city of our God;
He whose word cannot be broken formed thee for His
own abode;
On the Rock of Ages founded, what can shake thy sure
repose?
With salvation's walls surrounded, thou mayst smile at all
thy foes.

See, the streams of living waters, springing from eternal
love,
Well supply thy sons and daughters, and all fear of want
remove:
Who can faint, while such a river ever flows their thirst to
assuage?
Grace which, like the Lord, the Giver, never fails from age
to age.

Round each habitation hovering, see the cloud and fire
appear
For a glory and a covering, showing that the Lord is near!
Glorious things of thee are spoken, Zion, city of our God;
He, whose word cannot be broken, formed thee for His
own abode.

**I** *Surrender All* is a nice change of pace after a week's singing of a solemn hymn of praise. This is a soft, gentle pledge of devotion and submission.

There will be no working through archaic lyrics here, no studying theology or doctrine. Yet this is no easy ditty either. Unadorned in its style and approach, this is one of those convicting texts that does not allow us to sing it lightly.

*I Surrender All* is so unequivocal that you may find yourself interrupting the hymn to examine your heart. Every word here is stark and unqualified. The author wrote it reflecting on his decision to give himself fully to evangelistic ministry. He had an encounter with God not unlike that of Dr. James Dobson's father.

Dr. Dobson tells the story of his father's deciding on a career as an artist, despite feeling the call of God on his life for the ministry. He was miserable for years until he answered that call. Judson Van DeVenter says he also struggled between becoming an artist or an evangelist, and that during the pivotal hour, he surrendered all.

# I Surrender All

*Judson W. Van DeVenter*

All to Jesus I surrender, all to Him I freely give;
I will ever love and trust Him, in His presence daily live.

*Refrain*:
I surrender all, I surrender all.
All to Thee, my blessed Savior, I surrender all.

All to Jesus I surrender, humbly at His feet I bow,
Worldly pleasures all forsaken, take me, Jesus, take me
   now.

*Refrain*

All to Jesus I surrender, make me, Savior, wholly Thine;
Let me feel the Holy Spirit, truly know that Thou art mine.

*Refrain*

All to Jesus I surrender, Lord, I give myself to Thee;
Fill me with Thy love and power, let Thy blessing fall on
   me.

*Refrain*

**A**natural follow-up to *I Surrender All* is the lighter and brighter *O Happy Day*. Again, we're not dealing with heavy theology here, but the choice sentiments expressed are as encouraging to the singer as to the Object of his praise.

It's hard to have a bad day when you've begun with this song. "O happy bond, that seals my vows to Him who merits all my love!"

Philip Doddridge reportedly based the hymn on 2 Chronicles 15:15, "And all Judah rejoiced at the oath: for they had sworn with all their heart, and sought Him with their whole desire; and He was found of them: and the Lord gave them rest round about."

A verse seldom found in modern hymnals goes like this:

> High Heav'n that heard the solemn vow,
> That vow renewed shall daily hear;
> Till in life's latest hour I bow, and bless in
> death a bond so dear.

# O Happy Day
*Philip Doddridge*

O happy day that fixed my choice on Thee, my Savior and
my God!
Well may this glowing heart rejoice, and tell its raptures
all abroad.

*Refrain*:
Happy day, happy day, when Jesus washed my sins away!
He taught me how to watch and pray, and live rejoicing
ev'ry day;
Happy day, happy day, when Jesus washed my sins away!

O happy bond, that seals my vows to Him who merits all
my love!
Let cheerful anthems fill His house, while to that sacred
shrine I move.

*Refrain*

'Tis done: the great transaction's done; I am my Lord's,
and He is mine;
He drew me, and I followed on, charmed to confess the
voice divine.

*Refrain*

Now rest, my long divided heart; fixed on this blissful
center, rest;
Nor ever from my Lord depart, with Him of ev'ry good
possessed.

*Refrain*

# 6

*I Sing the Mighty Power of God*
*Nearer My God, to Thee*
*For the Beauty of the Earth*
*All Hail the Power of Jesus' Name*

**Y**ou've probably noticed by now that I like to begin each four-hymn bloc with an anthem praising God for His attributes. *I Sing the Mighty Power of God* fits perfectly that pattern.

Isaac Watts celebrates God's power, wisdom, goodness, creativity, and omnipresence. "While all that borrows life from Thee is ever in Thy care, and everywhere that man can be, Thou, God, art present there."

It is said that the author, who also penned *When I Survey the Wondrous Cross* and *O God, Our Help in Ages Past,* was frail, sickly, and grotesque in appearance. He was short with a huge head and a long, crooked nose. Yet what a man of God and of beautiful poetry! He is known as the father of English hymnody. Though he never married, he was especially fond of children, writing poems for and about them.

Though this is another of those majestic worship anthems, I enjoy singing it slowly and quietly for a reflective change of pace.

# I Sing the Mighty Power of God
### Isaac Watts

I sing the mighty power of God, that made the mountains
    rise;
That spread the flowing seas abroad, and built the lofty
    skies.
I sing the wisdom that ordained the sun to rule the day;
The moon shines full at His command, and all the stars
    obey.

I sing the goodness of the Lord, that filled the earth with
    food;
He formed the creatures with His word, and then
    pronounced them good.
Lord, how Thy wonders are displayed, where'er I turn my
    eye:
If I survey the ground I tread, or gaze upon the sky!

There's not a plant or flower below, but makes Thy
    glories known;
And clouds arise, and tempests blow, by order from Thy
    throne;
While all that borrows life from Thee is ever in Thy care,
And everywhere that man can be, Thou, God, art present
    there.

**A** friend of mine likes to dream up silly inventions. He never produces them, but they are interesting. For instance, he wanted to equip cars with hidden tape machines that played different songs depending on how fast the driver was going.

He had a list of mellow tunes for the lower speeds, but as the speedometer edged over the legal limit, the driver would hear *When the Roll Is Called Up Yonder,* and if he sped up, he would hear *Nearer, My God, to Thee*!

Of course, once you're exposed to something as ridiculous as that, you can't hear the song or even its title without a smile, but I still appreciate this hymn. Some say it is the finest hymn ever written by a woman.

Ironically, Sarah Adams was a Unitarian at the time of the writing, though there is evidence she was saved later in life and became a member of a Baptist church. The hymn is clearly based on Jacob's Old Testament vision. Note the second line of the fourth verse: "Out of my stony griefs, Bethel I'll raise."

Bethel means "house of God." When we sing hymns of devotion to Him, He dwells with us. Scripture says He inhabits the praise of His people.

# Nearer, My God, to Thee

*Sarah F. Adams*

Nearer, my God, to Thee, nearer to Thee!
E'en though it be a cross that raiseth me;
Still all my song shall be, nearer, my God to Thee,
Nearer, my God, to Thee, nearer to Thee.

Though like the wanderer, the sun gone down,
Darkness be over me, my rest a stone;
Yet in my dreams I'd be nearer, my God, to Thee,
Nearer, my God, to Thee, nearer to Thee.

There let the way appear steps unto heaven;
All that Thou sendest me in mercy given;
Angels to beckon me nearer, my God, to Thee,
Nearer, my God, to Thee, nearer to Thee.

Then, with my waking thoughts bright with Thy praise,
Out of my stony griefs, Bethel I'll raise;
So by my woes to be nearer, my God, to Thee,
Nearer, my God, to Thee, nearer to Thee.

Or if on joyful wing, cleaving the sky,
Sun, moon, and stars forgot, upward I fly,
Still all my song shall be nearer, my God, to Thee,
Nearer, my God, to Thee, nearer to Thee.

**F**or *the Beauty of the Earth* is a hymn of praise and thanks to God for nature, for family, for friends, for love, and for "all gentle thoughts and mild," which seems to cover everything.

But Folliott S. Pierpoint finishes by also praising God for "Thy Church," and four times refers to God as Lord of all.

You might enjoy one of the several verses not included in most modern hymnals, which also thanks God for Himself:

> For Thyself, best Gift Divine! To our race so
>     freely given;
> For that great, great love of Thine, peace on
>     earth, and joy in heaven.
> Lord of all, to Thee we raise this our hymn
>     of grateful praise.

Another variation on this and any of the other corporate hymns of worship included here is to change the plural pronouns to singular. Thus the last line of each verse would be sung, "Lord of all, to Thee I raise this my hymn of grateful praise."

# For the Beauty of the Earth

*Folliott S. Pierpoint*

For the beauty of the earth, for the glory of the skies,
For the love which from our birth over and around us lies,
Lord of all, to Thee we raise this our hymn of grateful
  praise.

For the beauty of each hour of the day and of the night,
Hill and vale, and tree, and flower, sun and moon and stars
  of light,
Lord of all, to Thee we raise this our hymn of grateful
  praise.

For the joy of human love, brother, sister, parent, child,
Friends on earth, and friends above, for all gentle thoughts
  and mild,
Lord of all, to Thee we raise this our hymn of grateful
  praise.

For Thy Church that evermore lifteth holy hands above,
Offering up on every shore Her pure sacrifice of love,
Lord of all, to Thee we raise this our hymn of grateful
  praise.

**I**'m hardly alone in listing *All Hail the Power* among my favorite anthems. Few hymns are as impressive or as thrilling when sung in a robust crowd. Even the repetition seems only to make more meaningful the beautiful phrasing. Indeed, we "crown Him Lord of all" no fewer than eight times in four verses.

I've tried slowing this one down, which seems to add to the regal, aristocratic bearing of it; but somehow it doesn't work for me when sung softly. There's something about the structure and lyric that begs for full voice.

Let it ring.

# All Hail the Power

*Edward Perronet*

All hail the power of Jesus' name! Let angels prostrate fall;
Bring forth the royal diadem, and crown Him Lord of all;
Bring forth the royal diadem, and crown Him Lord of all!

Ye chosen seed of Israel's race, ye ransomed from the fall,
Hail Him who saves you by His grace, and crown Him
Lord of all;
Hail Him who saves you by His grace, and crown Him
Lord of all!

Let every kindred, every tribe, on this terrestrial ball,
To Him all majesty ascribe, and crown Him Lord of all;
To Him all majesty ascribe, and crown Him Lord of all!

O that with yonder sacred throng we at His feet may fall!
We'll join the everlasting song, and crown Him Lord of all;
We'll join the everlasting song, and crown Him Lord of all!

# 7

*Love Divine, All Loves Excelling*
*Redeemed, How I Love to Proclaim It*
*Crown Him with Many Crowns*
*Come, Thou Fount*

**C**harles Wesley wrote 6,500 hymns, several more famous than *Love Divine, All Loves Excelling.* For instance, he wrote *O, For a Thousand Tongues to Sing; Jesus, Lover of My Soul; Christ the Lord Is Risen Today;* and *Hark! The Herald Angels Sing.*

He and his brother John, leading Methodists in eighteenth-century England, were considered renegades by the Anglican Church. Today we see Methodists as a quiet, mainstream, Protestant denomination. We have little concept of how they were persecuted two hundred years ago, their evangelists run out of town for heresy, their converts tormented and beaten, their homes looted.

For Wesley to produce a hymn as beautiful as this in spite of such turmoil makes it all the more amazing. He wrote hymns on every conceivable scriptural truth, and this one stands as a shining example of his view of the unconditional love of God.

# Love Divine, All Loves Excelling

*Charles Wesley*

Love divine, all loves excelling, joy of heaven, to earth
    come down;
Fix in us Thy humble dwelling; All Thy faithful mercies
    crown.
Jesus, Thou art all compassion, pure, unbounded love
    Thou art;
Visit us with Thy salvation; enter in our trembling heart.

Breathe, O breathe Thy loving Spirit into every troubled
    breast!
Let us all in Thee inherit, let us find that second rest.
Take away our bent to sinning, Alpha and Omega be;
End of faith, as its beginning, set our hearts at liberty.

Come, almighty to deliver, let us all Thy life receive;
Suddenly return, and never, nevermore Thy temple leave:
Thee we would be always blessing, serve Thee as Thy
    hosts above,
Pray, and praise Thee without ceasing, glory in Thy
    perfect love.

Finish then Thy new creation, pure and spotless let us be;
Let us see Thy great salvation perfectly restored in Thee:
Changed from glory into glory, till in heaven we take our
    place,
Till we cast our crowns before Thee, lost in wonder, love,
    and praise.

**F**ast forward a hundred years from Wesley to the time of the beloved, blind poetess Fanny J. Crosby. Her work and spirit are so much with us in worship services today that it's hard to believe she's been with the Lord for nearly seventy-five years. She wrote more than eight thousand songs.

As a child Fanny wrote that she would not wallow in self-pity because of her blindness, and by adulthood she chided someone who felt sorry for her: "Had it been up to me, I would have *asked* to have been born blind. This way, Jesus will be the first face I ever see."

That's why she could write such rousing hymns of praise as *Redeemed.* When she says she loves to proclaim it, she means it. "His child, and forever, I am."

We can say with her, "I sing for I cannot be silent; His love is the theme of my song."

# Redeemed, How I Love to Proclaim It

*Fanny J. Crosby*

Redeemed how I love to proclaim it! Redeemed by the
blood of the Lamb;
Redeemed through His infinite mercy, His child and
forever, I am.

*Refrain*:
Redeemed, redeemed, redeemed by the blood of the
Lamb;
Redeemed, redeemed, His child, and forever, I am.

Redeemed and so happy in Jesus, no language my rapture
can tell;
I know that the light of His presence with me doth
continually dwell.

*Refrain*

I think of my blessed Redeemer, I think of Him all the day
long;
I sing, for I cannot be silent; His love is the theme of my
song.

*Refrain*

I know I shall see in His beauty The King in whose law I
delight;
Who lovingly guardeth my footsteps, and giveth me songs
in the night.

*Refrain*

**W**hen I sang *Crown Him with Many Crowns* in church as a child, I thought the line, "Awake, my soul, and sing. . . ." had to do with getting up in the morning. I might have been bleary-eyed and would rather have stayed in bed. But the other words to this hymn, which also meant little to me as a youngster, implanted themselves on my brain so I could study and understand and enjoy them as an adult.

I especially enjoy the line, "Hark! how the heavenly anthem drowns all music but its own."

This is another of those hymns that can be sung at different paces, but which don't lend themselves to changes in volume. Rather, *Crown Him* . . . builds with pomp, the second half of each verse making you want to stand to sing.

# Crown Him with Many Crowns

*Matthew Bridges and Godfrey Thring*

Crown Him with many crowns, the Lamb upon His
   throne;
Hark! how the heavenly anthem drowns all music but its
   own!
Awake, my soul, and sing of Him who died for thee,
And hail Him as thy matchless King through all eternity.

Crown Him the Son of God before the worlds began,
And ye, who tread where He hath trod, crown Him the
   Son of man;
Who every grief hath known that wrings the human
   breast,
And takes and bears them for His own, that all in Him may
   rest.

Crown Him the Lord of life, who triumphed o'er the
   grave,
And rose victorious in the strife for those He came to
   save;
His glories now we sing who died, and rose on high,
Who died, eternal life to bring, and lives that death may
   die.

Crown Him the Lord of love! Behold His hands and side,
Rich wounds, yet visible above, in beauty glorified:
All hail, Redeemer, hail! For Thou hast died for me:
Thy praise shall never, never fail throughout eternity.

**T**he second phrase of *Come, Thou Fount* could have been used as the title to this book: Tune My Heart to Sing Thy Grace.

Most of the hymns in this volume contain archaic language, but this one has a most confusing phrase: "here I raise mine Ebenezer. . . ." The expression comes from 1 Samuel 7:12, where the Ebenezer was symbol of the faithfulness of God.

The writer of the hymn, Robert Robinson, turned to Christ from a life of sin as a young man at a George Whitefield meeting. He eventually entered the ministry as a Methodist but later became a Baptist preacher before lapsing into sin again.

This hymn, written when he was a fairly young Christian, darkly predicts that progression: "Prone to wander, Lord, I feel it, prone to leave the God I love." Our prayer should be all the more earnest: "Here's my heart, O take and seal it; seal it for Thy courts above."

# Come, Thou Fount

*Robert Robinson*

Come, Thou Fount of every blessing, tune my heart to
    sing Thy grace;
Streams of mercy, never ceasing, call for songs of loudest
    praise.
Teach me some melodious sonnet, sung by flaming
    tongues above;
Praise the mount—I'm fixed upon it—mount of Thy
    redeeming love.

Here I raise mine Ebenezer; higher by Thy help I'm come;
And I hope, by Thy good pleasure, safely to arrive at
    home.
Jesus sought me when a stranger, wandering from the fold
    of God;
He, to rescue me from danger, interposed His precious
    blood.

O to grace how great a debtor daily I'm constrained to be!
Let Thy goodness, like a fetter, bind my wandering heart
    to Thee:
Prone to wander, Lord, I feel it, prone to leave the God I
    love;
Here's my heart, O take and seal it; seal it for Thy courts
    above.

# 8

*O Worship the King*
*Fairest Lord Jesus*
*I Will Sing of My Redeemer*
*Savior, Like a Shepherd Lead Us*

**O***Worship the King* has been called a model worship anthem. You'll find yourself able to sing it from memory, even the second and third verses, after just a day or two.

The metaphors for God are varied and august: King, Shield, Defender, Ancient of Days, Maker, Redeemer, and Friend. Singing this magnificent hymn is like taking a trip through Scripture.

Experiment with changing the plural pronouns to singular for a change of pace. In the last verse, that would require changing *children* to *child* and holding the note where the second syllable would have been, along with changing *we* and *our* to *I* and *my*.

# O Worship the King
### Robert Grant

O worship the King, all glorious above,
O gratefully sing His power and His love;
Our Shield and Defender, the Ancient of Days,
Pavilioned in splendor, and girded with praise.

O tell of His might, O sing of His grace,
Whose robe is the light, whose canopy space.
His chariots of wrath the deep thunder clouds form,
And dark is His path on the wings of the storm.

Thy bountiful care what tongue can recite?
It breathes in the air, it shines in the light,
It streams from the hills, it descends to the plain,
And sweetly distills in the dew and the rain.

Frail children of dust, and feeble as frail,
In Thee do we trust, nor find Thee to fail;
Thy mercies how tender! how firm to the end!
Our Maker, Defender, Redeemer and Friend.

**T**here is almost a lullaby quality to the music of *Fairest Lord Jesus.* It's perfect for singing as a slow, quiet prayer.

I treasure the lovely phrasing and the way the tune inconspicuously builds drama. Jesus is compared with all the beauty of the earth and is found fairer, purer, and brighter. The first verse calls him "Thou of God and man the Son," while the last calls Him "Son of God and Son of Man."

If the tune is too familiar or becomes so after a few days, try simply reading this prayer to God. It is pure worship. "Glory and honor, praise, adoration, now and forever more be Thine."

# Fairest Lord Jesus
*From the German, 17th Century*

Fairest Lord Jesus! Ruler of all nature,
O Thou of God and man the Son!
Thee will I cherish, Thee will I honor,
Thou, my soul's Glory, Joy, and Crown!

Fair are the meadows, fairer still the woodlands,
Robed in the blooming garb of spring:
Jesus is fairer, Jesus is purer,
Who makes the woeful heart to sing.

Fair is the sunshine, fairer still the moonlight,
And all the twinkling starry host:
Jesus shines brighter, Jesus shines purer,
Than all the angels heaven can boast.

Beautiful Savior! Lord of the nations!
Son of God and Son of Man!
Glory and honor, praise, adoration,
Now and forever more be Thine!

**I** *Will Sing of My Redeemer* was written by my favorite hymnist, Philip P. Bliss. His *It Is Well With My Soul* is my most cherished gospel song, though because it is not designed to sing directly to God, it does not fit the criteria for this volume.

Bliss, though he died at just thirty-eight, wrote several other widely favored hymns, including *Let the Lower Lights Be Burning; Whosoever Will;* and *Wonderful Words of Life.*

*My Redeemer* is no theological tome, but it is profound in its simplicity, telling the story of redemption in straightforward language. The refrain is a marvelous outline of the spiritual transaction Christ made for us on the cross (purchased me, sealed my pardon, paid the debt, made me free).

# I Will Sing of My Redeemer
### *Philip P. Bliss*

I will sing of my Redeemer, and His wondrous love to me;
On the cruel cross He suffered, from the curse to set me
free.

*Refrain*:
Sing, oh, sing of my Redeemer, with His blood He
purchased me,
On the cross He sealed my pardon, paid the debt, and
made me free.

I will tell the wondrous story, how my lost estate to save,
In His boundless love and mercy, He the ransom freely
gave.

*Refrain*

I will praise my dear Redeemer, His triumphant power I'll
tell,
How the victory He giveth over sin, and death, and hell.

*Refrain*

I will sing of my Redeemer, and His heavenly love to me;
He from death to life hath brought me, Son of God, with
Him to be.

*Refrain*

**T**he image of Jesus Christ as a shepherd was impressed upon me at a young age. Two pictures hung on the wall at the front of our sanctuary—on the left Jesus praying in the garden, and on the right Jesus carrying a sheep on his shoulders.

As a youngster I mistook the painting on the left as God the Father, but no explanation was necessary for the other. I knew the story of the shepherd who had gone looking for one lost sheep out of a hundred, for each was precious to him.

As the baby of the family I identified with that sheep, and though I don't believe Scripture indicates this, I always assumed the lost sheep was a young one. Otherwise, why would he be lost?

Sometimes late at night I heard my mother playing the piano and singing. When she sang *Savior, Like a Shepherd Lead Us,* it nearly made me cry, but not from unhappiness. I was too young to understand the emotion, but now I know I simply adored the idea of having my own Shepherd—the good, the great Shepherd.

# Savior, Like a Shepherd Lead Us

*Attr. to Dorothy A. Thrupp*

Savior, like a shepherd lead us, Much we need Thy tender
care;
In Thy pleasant pastures feed us, For our use Thy folds
prepare:
Blessed Jesus, blessed Jesus, Thou hast bought us, Thine
we are;
Blessed Jesus, blessed Jesus, Thou hast bought us, Thine
we are.

We are Thine, do thou befriend us, Be the guardian of our
way;
Keep Thy flock, from sin defend us, Seek us when we go
astray:
Blessed Jesus, blessed Jesus, Hear, O hear us when we
pray;
Blessed Jesus, blessed Jesus, Hear, O hear us when we
pray.

Thou hast promised to receive us, Poor and sinful though
we be;
Thou hast mercy to relieve us, Grace to cleanse, and
pow'r to free:
Blessed Jesus, blessed Jesus, Early let us turn to Thee;
Blessed Jesus, blessed Jesus, Early let us turn to Thee.

Early let us seek Thy favor, Early let us do Thy will;
Blessed Lord and only Savior, With Thy love our bosoms
fill:
Blessed Jesus, blessed Jesus, Thou hast loved us, love us
still;
Blessed Jesus, blessed Jesus, Thou hast loved us, love us
still.

# 9

*Have Thine Own Way, Lord*
*Jesus, Keep Me Near the Cross*
*My Faith Looks Up to Thee*
*My Life, My Love, I Give to Thee*

**H**ave *Thine Own Way, Lord* is another of those hymns that cannot be sung glibly. It's a plain, unadorned tune, but the sentiments are sobering.

The first verse uses the traditional potter and clay metaphor and the subsequent verses ask that the Lord "wash me," "touch me," "help me," "heal me," "hold sway over me," "fill me," and "live in me."

It takes true faith to believe that God cares more about us than we do ourselves. We always fear that if we leave God to His own way, He'll take away everything good and fun and comfortable in our lives and send us to a mud hut in the jungle.

Dear friends of ours are missionaries in a thatched roof hut in West Africa. When they're stateside on furlough, they can't wait to get "home." They wanted God to have His own way, He did, and they love His choice.

For you and me, His will may be different. But it's always best, as the cliché goes: God always saves His best for those who leave the choice to Him.

# Have Thine Own Way, Lord

*Adelaide A. Pollard*

Have Thine own way, Lord! Have Thine own way!
Thou art the Potter, I am the clay.
Mold me and make me after Thy will,
While I am waiting yielded and still.

Have Thine own way, Lord! Have Thine own way!
Search me and try me, Master to day!
Whiter than snow, Lord, wash me just now,
As in Thy presence humbly I bow.

Have Thine own way, Lord! Have Thine own way!
Wounded and weary, help me, I pray!
Power—all power—surely is Thine!
Touch me and heal me, Savior divine!

Have Thine own way, Lord! Have Thine own way!
Hold o'er my being absolute sway!
Fill with Thy Spirit till all shall see
Christ only, always, living in me!

**J**esus, *Keep Me Near the Cross* is another Fanny Crosby favorite. Again she thrills us with straightforward images: the precious fountain that is a "healing stream" and "flows from calvary's mountain," the Bright and Morning Star that "sheds its beams around me," the raptured soul that finds "rest beyond the river."

When I sing this insightful hymn I like to imagine Fanny Crosby on the "other side," having already reached that "golden strand just beyond the river." I just know she's bounding about the place, thrilled that her first and only sights were eternal.

The return of Christ and the centrality of the cross are paramount in her works. This hymn is another that can be simply spoken as a variation. Pray it to Christ.

# Jesus, Keep Me Near the Cross

*Fanny J. Crosby*

Jesus, keep me near the cross, There a precious fountain
Free to all, a healing stream, Flows from Calv'ry's
mountain.

*Refrain:*
In the cross, in the cross be my glory ever;
Till my raptured soul shall find rest beyond the river.

Near the cross, a trembling soul, love and mercy found me;
There the Bright and Morning Star sheds its beams around
me.

*Refrain*

Near the cross! O Lamb of God, bring its scenes before me;
Help me walk from day to day with its shadows o'er me.

*Refrain*

Near the cross I'll watch and wait, hoping, trusting ever,
Till I reach the golden strand just beyond the river.

*Refrain*

**B**oth Dr. George Sweeting and Dr. Warren Wiersbe are fond of saying that the Christian life can be called a series of new beginnings. It makes sense that they should agree. Both were pastors of effective churches—in fact, Wiersbe followed Sweeting at the historic Moody Memorial Church when Sweeting became president of the Moody Bible Institute in 1971. Both are authors and radio preachers. Both know the process of daily confession and recommitment.

Ray Palmer, in the meditative *My Faith Looks Up to Thee,* begins with the plea, "take all my guilt away, O let me from this day be wholly Thine!"

After guilt in the first verse, Palmer admits to a fainting heart in the second, treading a dark maze and grieving in darkness and sorrow in the third, and fear and distrust in the fourth.

Can you identify with this the way I can? This is an earthy, almost gritty hymn of stark reality, acknowledging the weak, frail human frame for what it is. Yet there is victory here too, especially in the last line. Enjoy.

# My Faith Looks Up to Thee
### *Ray Palmer*

My faith looks up to Thee, Thou lamb of Calvary,
Savior divine!
Now hear me while I pray, take all my guilt away,
O let me from this day be wholly Thine!

May Thy rich grace impart strength to my fainting heart,
My zeal inspire;
As Thou hast died for me, O may my love to Thee
Pure, warm, and changeless be, a living fire!

While life's dark maze I tread, and griefs around me
    spread,
Be Thou my guide;
Bid darkness turn to day, wipe sorrow's tears away,
Nor let me ever stray from Thee aside.

When ends life's transient dream, when death's cold,
    sullen stream
Shall o'er me roll;
Blest Savior, then, in love, fear and distrust remove;
O bear me safe above, a ransomed soul!

There is a frank, unpretentious, balanced structure in *My Life, My Love I Give to Thee,* in which the writer contrasts his wish to give his own life to Christ with the character of the faithful One who died for him.

This hymn could be called a Christian's pledge of allegiance put to music. Its slightly archaic language is easily understood and sets forth a pure, heartfelt covenant.

The one who wrote this, and the one who would sing it, is saying to God, "You have my all, I want to be forever faithful, I'll live for you happily, I'll trust in You."

The One credited for that, the acknowledged Source of the strength to effect it, is—of course—"the Lamb of God who died for me."

# My Life, My Love I Give to Thee
*Ralph E. Hudson*

My life, my love I give to Thee, Thou Lamb of God who
died for me;
O may I ever faithful be, my Savior and my God!

*Refrain*:
I'll live for Him who died for me, how happy then my life
shall be!
I'll live for Him who died for me, my Savior and my God.

I now believe Thou dost receive, for Thou hast died that I
might live;
And now henceforth I'll trust in Thee, my Savior and my
God.

*Refrain*

O Thou who died on Calvary, to save my soul and make
me free,
I'll consecrate my life to Thee, My Savior and my God!

*Refrain*

# 10

*Immortal, Invisible, God Only Wise*
*O For a Thousand Tongues to Sing*
*Come, Thou Almighty King*
*Blessed Assurance*

**W**alter C. Smith pours on the laurels to God in *Immortal, Invisible, God Only Wise.* The title is also the first phrase, and then Smith calls God blessed, glorious, almighty, victorious, unresting, unhasting, silent, not wanting, not wasting, ruling, just, good, loving, life giving, true, unchanging, great, and adored of angels.

It's difficult to imagine the writer coming up with so many superlatives, but somehow he makes them work in this regal hymn of worship and praise.

The only problem I have in singing this one is that no matter how slowly you take it, it's difficult to ponder the full meaning of each word. You almost have to stop singing after each word and ponder its ramifications.

Indeed, God is all this and more, and Smith must have felt inadequate at the end of the writing. He must have wished, as we do, that he could find enough words to do justice to the greatness of God.

But that's not to be in this lifetime. The heavenly chorus will have the glorified minds and bodies to do it, and *Immortal, Invisible...* will be only the beginning.

# Immortal, Invisible,
# God Only Wise
*Walter C. Smith*

Immortal, invisible, God only wise,
In light inaccessible hid from our eyes,
Most blessed, most glorious, the ancient of Days,
Almighty, victorious, Thy great name we praise.

Unresting, unhasting, and silent as light,
Nor wanting, nor wasting, Thou rulest in might;
Thy justice like mountains high soaring above
Thy clouds, which are fountains of goodness and love.

To all, life Thou givest, to both great and small,
In all life Thou livest, the true life of all.
We blossom and flourish as leaves on the tree,
And wither and perish—but naught changeth Thee.

Great Father of glory, pure Father of light,
Thine angels adore Thee, all veiling their sight;
All praise we would render; O help us to see
'Tis only the splendor of light hideth Thee!

**W**alter C. Smith's attempt to find enough accolades in the previous hymn is reflected in Charles Wesley's lament here. Have you ever shared his frustration and wished you had a thousand tongues to sing your great Redeemer's praise?

How do we go about getting a handle on the glories of our God and King, the triumphs of His grace?

Wesley, writer of 6,500 hymns, seeks God's assistance within the hymn "to spread through all the earth abroad, the honors of Thy name."

After two verses directed specifically to God, Wesley raises the banner for the name of Jesus, who charms fears and bids sorrows cease. He moves from there into a proclamation of the power of Christ's work on the cross.

Wesley reportedly wrote this hymn on the eleventh anniversary of his conversion experience. The final verse asks the deaf, the dumb, the blind, and the lame to hear, to speak, to see, and to leap for joy as "behold, your Savior comes."

# O for a Thousand Tongues
### Charles Wesley

O for a thousand tongues to sing my great Redeemer's
praise,
The glories of my God and King, the triumphs of His
grace.

My gracious Master and my God, assist me to proclaim,
To spread through all the earth abroad, the honors of Thy
name.

Jesus! the name that charms my fears, that bids my
sorrows cease;
'Tis music in the sinner's ears, 'tis life, and health, and
peace.

He breaks the power of canceled sin, He sets the prisoner
free;
His blood can make the foulest clean; His blood availed
for me.

Hear Him, ye deaf; His praise, ye dumb, your loosened
tongues employ;
Ye blind, behold your Savior come; and leap, ye lame, for
joy.

**T**hough the writer of *Come, Thou Almighty King* is unknown, he or she is another who asks God Himself to "help me Thy name to sing, help me to praise. . . ."

God is referred to here as the Almighty King, the Ancient of Days, the Incarnate Word, the Spirit of Holiness, the Holy Comforter, the Almighty, the Spirit of power, the great One in Three, and the Sovereign Majesty.

The writer also asks God to "reign over me, on me descend, and ne'er from me depart."

When this hymn first appeared anonymously in England in 1757, it was sung to the same tune we now use for *My Country, Tis of Thee.* I prefer the tune most associated with it now, but using various tunes is a good way to get a different perspective on lyrics. These are worth the meditation.

# Come, Thou Almighty King

*Source Unknown*

Come, Thou Almighty King, help us Thy name to sing,
Help us to praise: Father, all glorious, o'er all victorious,
Come, and reign over us, Ancient of Days.

Come, Thou Incarnate Word, gird on Thy mighty sword,
Our prayer attend: Come, and Thy people bless, and give
    Thy word success:
Spirit of Holiness, on us descend.

Come, Holy Comforter, Thy sacred witness bear
In this glad hour: Thou who almighty art, now rule in
    every heart,
And ne'er from us depart, Spirit of power.

To the great One in Three eternal praises be
Hence, evermore! His sovereign majesty may we in glory
    see,
And to eternity love and adore!

**B**y now you're aware that Fanny J. Crosby has more hymns in this collection than any other writer. Her *Blessed Assurance* is typically straightforward, biblically-based, and Christ-centered.

Some highbrow classical music lovers consider Crosby material Sunday schoolish and pedestrian, but I've been in worse company. I like Sunday school and regular people, and I know I would have loved to have known Fanny Crosby. She'll never be listed with Beethoven or Mozart, but more than seventy-five years after her death, she still speaks to me through her lyrics.

Her writing is unabashedly emotional. The refrain of *Blessed Assurance* could be the theme of her existence as she repeats, "This is my story, this is my song, praising my Savior all the day long."

I was a doubter as a child, not of the truth of the faith but of the validity of my conversion. I knew my imperfections, and my humanness dogged me. It wasn't until I was a college freshman that I really felt peace about my destiny, finally learning that the work had been done, that fact was fact regardless of my faith or the feeling that accompanied it.

To a person who has ever wondered about his eternal security, *Blessed Assurance* is blessed indeed.

# Blessed Assurance
*Fanny J. Crosby*

Blessed assurance, Jesus is mine! Oh, what a foretaste of
glory divine!
Heir of salvation, purchase of God, Born of His Spirit,
washed in His blood.

*Refrain:*
This is my story, this is my song, praising my Savior all the
day long;
This is my story, this is my song, praising my Savior all the
day long.

Perfect submission, perfect delight, visions of rapture now
burst on my sight;
Angels descending, bring from above echoes of mercy,
whispers of love.

*Refrain*

Perfect submission, all is at rest, I in my Savior am happy
and blest;
Watching and waiting, looking above, filled with His
goodness, lost in His love.

*Refrain*

# 11

*Spirit of God, Descend upon My Heart*
*Open My Eyes, That I May See*
*Sweet Hour of Prayer*
*And Can It Be That I Should Gain?*

*Spirit of God, Descend upon My Heart* can be sung only in quiet, reverential tones. It's the perfect hymn to celebrate Pentecost. This set of five verses is so rich and deep in imagery and truth that you might want to concentrate on a verse a day.

Many believe that the last line in the last verse is the most beautiful metaphor in hymnody: "My heart an altar, and Thy love the flame."

I remember clearly when the Spirit of God descended on my heart. I was a teenager, finally seeing my inconsistent Christian life for what it was: empty and phony. When I got right with God, confessed sin, and committed myself to live for Christ by God's grace, even if I had to stand alone, I felt the presence of Christ.

I was bolder in my witness, stronger in my resolve, eager to serve God and to see my friends come to Christ. That's when hymns like this one, which I had long considered outdated, slow, and boring, became as tasty to me as the meat of the Word.

# Spirit of God, Descend upon My Heart

### *George Croly*

Spirit of God, descend upon my heart;
Wean it from earth, through all its pulses move;
Stoop to my weakness, mighty as Thou art,
And make me love Thee as I ought to love.

I ask no dream, no prophet ecstasies,
No sudden rending of the veil of clay,
No angel visitant, no opening skies;
But take the dimness of my soul away.

Hast Thou not bid me love Thee, God and King?
All, all Thine own, soul, heart and strength and mind.
I see Thy cross—there teach my heart to cling:
O let me seek Thee, and O let me find.

Teach me to feel that Thou art always nigh;
Teach me the struggles of the soul to bear,
To check the rising doubt, the rebel sigh:
Teach me the patience of unanswered prayer.

Teach me to love Thee as Thine angels love,
One holy passion filling all my frame;
The baptism of the heaven descended Dove,
My heart an altar, and Thy love the flame.

**O**pen My Eyes . . . is a hymn with a tune and lyrics attractive to young people. The youth group I grew up with loved to sing this song, but it should never be considered exclusively for the young.

The hymn appeals to the senses (Open my eyes, open my ears, open my mouth), including the sense of touch ("Place in my hands the wonderful key that shall unclasp, and set me free.").

The convicting line of this hymn is "Silently now I wait for Thee, ready my God, Thy will to see. . . ." How often do we go to the Lord in prayer, say all that we want to say—including praise, confession, thanks, and requests—then say amen and leave?

Real prayer warriors know how to wait upon the Lord, to be still and know that He is God. That is the area of prayer I most struggle with. Maybe singing this hymn for a week will help implant the proper discipline.

# Open My Eyes, That I May See

*Clara H. Scott*

Open my eyes, that I may see glimpses of truth Thou hast
    for me;
Place in my hands the wonderful key that shall unclasp,
    and set me free.
Silently now I wait for Thee, ready, my God, Thy will to
    see;
Open my eyes, illumine me, Spirit divine!

Open my ears, that I may hear voices of truth Thou
    sendest clear;
And while the wavenotes fall on my ear, everything false
    will disappear.
Silently now I wait for Thee, ready, my God, Thy will to
    see;
Open my ears, illumine me, Spirit divine!

Open my mouth, and let me bear gladly the warm truth
    everywhere;
Open my heart, and let me prepare love with Thy
    children thus to share.
Silently now I wait for Thee, ready, my God, Thy will to
    see;
Open my heart, illumine me, Spirit divine!

**L**ike the previous hymn, *Sweet Hour of Prayer* speaks eloquently of two-way communication with God. As a child I thought this hymn referred to sixty minutes worth of praying, and I wondered if the writer knew our pastor. His congregational prayers were legendary. They were likely not ten minutes long, but to a six- or seven-year-old with a fidget and a mandate to both sit still and keep his eyes closed, that seemed an hour.

Of course I now realize that *hour* in this context means *time* or *season.* Here again we see prayer not represented solely as a vehicle for talking to God, but as an oasis from the world, calling us from care.

As sweet as is the hour of private communion with God, the writer also looks forward to that day when he sees his Savior face to face and can bid farewell to prayer. It's an interesting thought: there will be no prayer in heaven.

# Sweet Hour of Prayer
*William W. Walford*

Sweet hour of prayer, sweet hour of prayer, that calls me
from a world of care,
And bids me at my Father's throne make all my wants and
wishes known;
In seasons of distress and grief, my soul has often found
relief,
And oft escaped the tempter's snare, by thy return, sweet
hour of prayer.

Sweet hour of prayer, sweet hour of prayer, thy wings
shall my petition bear,
To Him whose truth and faithfulness engage the waiting
soul to bless;
And since He bids me seek His face, believe His word and
trust His grace,
I'll cast on Him my every care, and wait for thee, sweet
hour of prayer.

Sweet hour of prayer, sweet hour of prayer, may I thy
consolation share,
Till, from Mount Pisgah's lofty height, I view my home,
and take my flight:
This robe of flesh I'll drop, and rise to seize the everlasting
prize;
And shout, while passing through the air, farewell,
farewell, sweet hour of prayer!

**C**harles Wesley seems to take personal blame for the death of Christ on the cross in his hymn, *And Can It Be That I Should Gain?* He says, "Died He for me, who caused His pain? For me, who Him to death pursued?"

This is a model for us in seeing our guilt, not because of Adam's fall, not because we were born in sin—though we were. Rather, I must realize that if no one before me had fallen, I would have.

It's amazing that a writer with so many hymns to his credit can reach a height such as this. A work as imperial as this one can be sung quietly and prayerfully too, though my guess is you have never heard it rendered that way. It may seem strange at first, but try it.

If you can hear the rolling basses, throw them in, sing all the parts. *And Can It Be* . . . has long been one of my favorite congregational hymns, but it is also wonderful sung at a different pace, in private.

# And Can It Be That I Should Gain?

*Charles Wesley*

And can it be that I should gain an interest in the Savior's blood?
Died He for me, who caused His pain? For me, who Him to
death pursued?
Amazing love! how can it be that Thou, my God, shouldst die
for me?

*Refrain*:
Amazing love! how can it be that Thou, my God, shouldst die
for me?

'Tis mystery all! Th'Immortal dies! Who can explore His strange
design?
In vain the first-born seraph tries to sound the depths of love
divine!
'Tis mercy all! let earth adore, let angel minds inquire no more.

*Refrain*

He left His Father's throne above, so free, so infinite His grace;
Emptied Himself of all but love, and bled for Adam's helpless
race;
'Tis mercy all, immense and free; for, O my God, it found out
me.

*Refrain*

Long my imprisoned spirit lay fast bound in sin and nature's
night;
Thine eye diffused a quick'ning ray, I woke, the dungeon flamed
with light;
My chains fell off, my heart was free; I rose, went forth, and followed Thee.

*Refrain*

No condemnation now I dread; Jesus, and all in Him, is mine!
Alive in Him, my living Head, and clothed in righteousness
divine,
Bold I approach th'eternal throne, and claim the crown, thro'
Christ my own.

*Refrain*

# 12

*We Praise Thee, O God, Our Redeemer*
*Blessed Be the Name*
*Praise Ye the Lord, the Almighty*
*Thanks to God for My Redeemer*

**S**ing *We Praise Thee, O God* to the more popular tune of *We Gather Together.* Here is a hymn that can easily be made more personal by changing the *we, our,* and *us* to *I, my,* and *me.* The first line of the last verse may be changed from "With voices united our praises we offer," to "With others united my praises I offer."

The tune alone gives this a Thanksgiving feel, so perhaps it'll remind you, like me, of family reunions.

# We Praise Thee,
# O God Our Redeemer
*Julia C. Cory*

We praise Thee, O God, our Redeemer, Creator,
In grateful devotion our tribute we bring;
We lay it before Thee, we kneel and adore Thee,
We bless Thy holy name, glad praises we sing.

We worship Thee, God of our fathers, we bless Thee,
Through life's storm and tempest our guide hast Thou
    been;
When perils o'ertake us, Thou wilt not forsake us,
And with Thy help, O Lord, life's battles we win.

With voices united our praises we offer,
And gladly our songs of true worship we raise;
Our sins now confessing, we pray for Thy blessing:
To Thee, our great Redeemer, forever be praise.

**B**lessed Be the Name is fun to sing because of its familiar, sprightly tune. I enjoy singing the harmony to it, even privately. I know that sounds strange (but so does my singing).

In spite of the lightness of it, the truth rings clear in its repetitious refrain. I especially love the last verse, where some of the names of Christ—most often heard around Christmas—are included.

This hymn is neither deep nor difficult. It's almost as if this were designed to slide off the tongue. Yet it contains solid biblical doctrine. We see God reigning in majesty, giving His Son, redeeming man; see Jesus' name standing above all others; see Jesus exalted, at the Father's right hand, adored by angels, called Redeemer, Savior, Friend of man, Counselor, Prince of Peace, and Conqueror.

All this in four brief verses. Any writer appreciates such economy. And private singers will too.

# Blessed Be the Name

*W. H. Clark (Refrain, Ralph E. Hudson)*

All praise to Him who reigns above in majesty supreme,
Who gave His Son for man to die, that He might man
   redeem!

*Refrain:*
Blessed be the name, blessed be the name,
Blessed be the name of the Lord;
Blessed be the name, blessed be the name,
Blessed be the name of the Lord.

His name above all names shall stand, exalted more and
   more,
At God the Father's own right hand, where angel hosts
   adore.

*Refrain*

Redeemer, Savior, Friend of man once ruined by the fall,
Thou hast devised salvation's plan, for Thou hast died for
   all.

*Refrain*

His name shall be the Counsellor, the mighty Prince of
   Peace,
Of all earth's kingdoms Conqueror, whose reign shall
   never cease.

*Refrain*

**T**here is something reminiscent of Fanny Crosby in *Praise Ye the Lord, the Almighty,* yet it couldn't be. The writer, Joachim Neander lived thirty brief years in the second half of the seventeenth century. Miss Crosby died early in this century.

Yet in his lively hymn are the Crosbyesque, unambiguous words that describe the greatness of God and the writer's humble state before Him.

Though Neander died young, he earned a reputation as a scholar in several disciplines and was a Reformed Church pastor in Dusseldorf, Germany. He wrote sixty hymns and many tunes, but this is considered his finest.

# Praise Ye the Lord, the Almighty

*Joachim Neander*

Praise ye the Lord, the Almighty, the King of creation!
O my soul, praise Him, for He is my health and salvation!
All ye who hear, now to His temple draw near;
Join me in glad adoration!

Praise ye the Lord, who o'er all things so wondrously
   reigneth,
Shelters me under His wings, yea, so gently sustaineth!
Have I not seen how my desires e'er have been
Granted in what He ordaineth?

Praise ye the Lord, who with marvelous wisdom hath
   made me!
Decked me with health, and with loving hand guided and
   stayed me;
How oft in grief hath not He brought me relief,
Spreading His wings for to shade me!

Praise ye the Lord! O let all that is in me adore Him!
All that hath life and breath, come now with praises
   before Him!
Let the Amen sound from His people again:
Gladly for aye I adore Him.

**I**f you began going through this book at the beginning of the year and have sung a song for each week, you should be in your forty-eighth week. That will put you close to Thanksgiving.

What better hymn for this season than *Thanks to God for My Redeemer*? Sweden's August L. Storm has written a realistic verse that is more than simply a God-is-great-God-is-good sentiment. The thirty-two "thanks" are for everything from provisions and balmy springtime to dark and dreary fall and "what Thou dost deny."

This is an engaging kind of a writer, one who thanks God for pain and for pleasure, for joy and for sorrow, for roses and for thorns. Clearly this is a man who has been there, experiencing life in its fullest, good and bad. And isn't that the purest praise? The most honest?

He finishes by thanking God for heavenly peace, for hope in the tomorrow, and thanks through all eternity.

# Thanks to God for My Redeemer
*August L. Storm*

Thanks to God for my Redeemer, thanks for all Thou dost
provide!
Thanks for times now but a mem'ry, thanks for Jesus by
my side!
Thanks for pleasant, balmy springtime, thanks for dark and
dreary fall!
Thanks for tears by now forgotten, thanks for peace
within my soul!

Thanks for prayers that Thou hast answered, thanks for
what Thou dost deny!
Thanks for storms that I have weathered, thanks for all
Thou dost supply!
Thanks for pain and thanks for pleasure, thanks for
comfort in despair!
Thanks for grace that none can measure, thanks for love
beyond compare!

Thanks for roses by the wayside, thanks for thorns their
stems contain!
Thanks for homes and thanks for fireside, thanks for hope,
that sweet refrain!
Thanks for joy and thanks for sorrow, thanks for heav'nly
peace with Thee!
Thanks for hope in the tomorrow, thanks thro' all
eternity!

# 13

*Joyful, Joyful, We Adore Thee*
*Jesus, I Am Resting, Resting*
*Jesus, the Very Thought of Thee*
*Thou Didst Leave Thy Throne*

**J**oyful, Joyful, We Adore Thee cannot be sung without thinking of the masterpiece of music that has made it so poignant. Written by Ludwig van Beethoven long after he had become deaf, the tune was known around the world before it was associated with these lyrics by Henry van Dyke.

I've tried to sing this one slowly, but the tune is so reminiscent of sprightly harpsichords that the words begin to bounce, and suddenly I'm singing it the way it was meant to be sung—at least in style.

It is said that van Dyke himself characterized the hymn as a collection of common Christian feelings and added that it may be sung by people who know that science cannot destroy their faith, nor any earthly revolution threaten the kingdom of God.

I'm chagrined to admit that I was a teenager before I understood the title and the first line. Somehow I had mistaken *Joyful* as another name for God, finally realizing that it, of course, refers to our mind-set as we adore Him.

# Joyful, Joyful, We Adore Thee

*Henry van Dyke*

Joyful, joyful, we adore Thee, God of glory, Lord of love;
Hearts unfold like flowers before Thee, praising Thee
    their sun above.
Melt the clouds of sin and sadness, drive the dark of doubt
    away;
Giver of immortal gladness, fill us with the light of day!

All Thy works with joy surround Thee, earth and heaven
    reflect Thy rays,
Stars and angels sing around Thee, center of unbroken
    praise:
Field and forest, vale and mountain, blooming meadow,
    flashing sea,
Chanting bird and flowing fountain, call us to rejoice in
    Thee.

Thou art giving and forgiving, ever blessing, ever blest,
Wellspring of the joy of living, ocean-depth of happy rest!
Thou our Father, Christ our Brother, all who live in love
    are Thine:
Teach us how to love each other, lift us to the Joy Divine.

Mortals join the mighty chorus, which the morning stars
    began;
Father-love is reigning o'er us, brother-love binds man to
    man.
Ever singing, march we onward, victor in the midst of
    strife;
Joyful music lifts us sunward in the triumph song of life.

**C**ollege students often find novel ways to inform their dorm mates where they are. When I was a freshman at Moody Bible Institute in the late 1960s, a friend of mine hung a multiple choice list on his door. Some of the offerings included Gone Fishing, In the Prayer Room, On a Date, Studying—Please Do Not Disturb, and my favorite, I Am Resting, Resting.

It's only when we get out of high school and begin to notice the speedy passage of time that we realize how important and inviting rest is. Is there anything more delicious than a much needed nap on a Sunday afternoon?

Now combine that comfortable feeling with the security of finding true, pure rest in Jesus. I particularly love the last three lines of the third verse, which are about Christ's love, so pure, so changeless that it satisfies my heart's deepest longings, meets and supplies its every need, and compasses me round with blessings. "Thine is love indeed!"

# Jesus, I Am Resting, Resting
## *Jean S. Pigott*

Jesus, I am resting, resting in the joy of what Thou art;
I am finding out the greatness of Thy loving heart.
Thou hast bid me gaze upon Thee, and Thy beauty fills my
soul,
For by Thy transforming power, Thou hast made me
whole.

*Refrain*:
Jesus, I am resting, resting, in the joy of what Thou art,
I am finding out the greatness of Thy loving heart.

Oh, how great Thy loving kindness, vaster, broader than
the sea!
Oh, how marvelous Thy goodness, lavished all on me!
Yes, I rest in Thee, Beloved, know what wealth of grace is
Thine,
Know Thy certainty of promise, and have made it mine.

*Refrain*

Simply trusting Thee, Lord Jesus, I behold Thee as Thou
art,
And Thy love, so pure, so changeless, satisfies my heart;
Satisfies its deepest longings, meets, supplies its every
need,
Compasseth me round with blessings: Thine is love
indeed!

*Refrain*

Ever lift Thy face upon me, as I work and wait for Thee;
Resting 'neath Thy smile, Lord Jesus, earth's dark shadows
flee.
Brightness of my Father's glory, sunshine of my Father's
face,
Keep me ever trusting, resting, fill me with Thy grace.

*Refrain*

135

**B**ernard of Clairvaux was apparently one of the few devout men of God during the Middle Ages, a period when the church of Christ was largely corrupt and of ill repute.

The words to his beautiful *Jesus, the Very Thought of Thee* are simple and straightforward and seem written just for the music we so often associate with it. Here is a hymn perfect for private devotions. It can be sung slowly, prayerfully, quietly, and with deep meaning.

Bernard calls Jesus the hope of every contrite heart, the joy of the meek, kind to the fallen, good to the seeking, and what to those who find? "Ah! this. Nor tongue nor pen can show, the love of Jesus, what it is, none but His loved ones know."

As loved ones of His, we know what the love of Jesus is. And that's what makes hymns like this so precious to us.

# Jesus, the Very Thought of Thee

*Bernard of Clairvaux*

Jesus, the very thought of Thee with sweetness fills my
  breast;
But sweeter far Thy face to see, and in Thy presence rest.

Nor voice can sing, nor heart can frame, nor can the
  memory find
A sweeter sound than Thy blest name, O Savior of
  mankind!

O Hope of every contrite heart, O Joy of all the meek,
To those who fall, how kind Thou art! How good to those
  who seek!

But what to those who find? Ah! this. Nor tongue nor pen
  can show,
The love of Jesus, what it is, none but His loved ones
  know.

The only Christmas carol in this collection is *Thou Didst Leave Thy Throne* by Emily E. S. Elliott. I selected it because it is written directly to Jesus and can be sung as a song-prayer. The tune is so familiar after years of Christmas pageants, services, and songfests that you may want to simply recite it. This is a fitting way to close the volume, because of the petition at the end of each verse. After an outline of the nativity and purpose of God's coming to earth in the form of man, each verse ends, "O come to my heart, Lord Jesus! There is room in my heart for Thee."

A friend of mine wrote a touching short story for *Guideposts* magazine several years ago, in which a retarded boy plays the part of the innkeeper in Bethlehem. In his pivotal scene he tells Mary and Joseph, "No, there is no room!" But as they trudge away, looking so sad, he blurts, "Come back! You can have my room!"

I trust you've been able to use the hymns in this volume to express to God your willingness to make room in your heart for Him.

# Thou Didst Leave Thy Throne

*Emily E. S. Elliott*

Thou didst leave Thy throne and Thy kingly crown
When Thou camest to earth for me;
But in Bethlehem's home was there found no room
For Thy holy nativity:
O come to my heart, Lord Jesus! There is room in my
  heart for Thee.

Heaven's arches rang when the angels sang,
Proclaiming Thy royal degree;
But in lowly birth didst Thou come to earth,
And in great humility:
O come to my heart, Lord Jesus! There is room in my
  heart for Thee.

Thou camest, O Lord, with the living Word
That should set Thy people free;
But with mocking scorn, and with crown of thorn,
They bore Thee to Calvary:
O come to my heart, Lord Jesus! There is room in my
  heart for Thee.

When the heavens shall ring, and the angels sing,
At Thy coming to victory,
Let Thy voice call me home, saying, "Yet there is room,
There is room at My side for thee:"
My heart shall rejoice, Lord, Jesus! When Thou comest
  and callest for me.

# Index of Hymns

# Index of Authors

Moody Press, a ministry of the Moody Bible Institute, is designed for education, evangelization, and edification. If we may assist you in knowing more about Christ and the Christian life, please write us without obligation: Moody Press, c/o MLM, Chicago, Illinois 60610.